Irrevocable,
Unalterable...

# Laws
## of Dating

**Pacific Press® Publishing Association**
Nampa, Idaho
Oshawa, Ontario, Canada
www.pacificpress.com

Cover design by Gerald Lee Monks
Cover design resources from dreamstime.com
Inside design by Steve Lanto

Copyright © 2007 by
Pacific Press® Publishing Association
Printed in the United States of America
All rights reserved

Additional copies of this book are available by calling toll-free
1-800-765-6955 or by visiting
www.AdventistBookCenter.com

Scriptures quoted from the NIV are from the HOLY BIBLE, NEW INTERNATIONAL VERSION®. Copyright © 1973, 1978, 1984 by the International Bible Society. Used by permission of Zondervan Bible Publishers. All rights reserved.

Scriptures quoted from NKJV are from The New King James Version, copyright © 1979, 1980, 1982, Thomas Nelson, Inc., Publishers.

Library of Congress Cataloging-in-Publication Data

Tucker, Mike (Michael Duane)
Laws of dating : the irrefutable, irrevocable, unalterable / Mike Tucker.
    p. cm.
ISBN-13: 978-0-8163-2247-3 (pbk.)
ISBN-10: 0-8163-2247-3
1. Single people—Conduct of life. 2. Dating (Social customs)—Religious aspects—Christianity. 3. Mate selection—Religious aspects—Christianity. 4. Marriage—Religious aspects—Christianity.
I. Title.
BV4596.S5T83 2007
241'.6765--dc22
                                                            2007031132

07 08 09 10 11 • 5 4 3 2 1

# Contents

Why Date? ....................................................................... 5

The Laws ......................................................................... 9

Breaking Up Is Hard to Do ........................................... 46

True Love ....................................................................... 51

Finding True Love .......................................................... 55

Bringing It All Together ................................................. 61

# Why Date?

A band named the Poverty Neck Hillbillies has recorded a song about how hard it is to find one's true love. The lyrics say that the listener could "spend the night waiting for a Prince Charming to come along," but if she'll look around with a critical eye, she'll likely conclude that she'll be "waiting a long, long time." Then the singer offers himself as a second-rate fill-in:

> I might not be Mr. Right, but, baby, we could have some fun tonight.
> I might not be Mr. Right, but I'm Mr. Right Now.

I've written this book in the hopes of helping you avoid Mr. or Ms. Right Now as you wait for your Mr. Right or Ms. Right.

If you are like most people today, you've almost given up on the thought of having a healthy, fulfilling relationship. Many of the dating relationships you've experienced have been disastrous. And while dating is difficult, marriage seems like an absolute impossibility. Maybe your parents' marriage has been a nightmare and your friends' marriages don't seem much better. Or if your parents have a healthy marriage, you may have come to believe that a marriage like theirs isn't possible today—people like your parents just don't exist anymore.

America's high divorce rate appears to confirm your suspicions: If such a thing as a quality relationship or marriage actually exists, it's rare enough to be listed as an endangered species. So, looking for the perfect mate seems to be a waste of time, and you may well be tempted to settle for Mr. or Ms. Right Now.

While I know I run the risk of sounding hopelessly out of touch with reality, I truly believe that you can have a quality dating experience. More than that, I believe you can find your Mr. Right or Ms. Right and experience a satisfying, joyful, and lasting marriage.

However, accomplishing this rather lofty goal will take work and discipline. If you are to achieve something as improbable as a quality relationship, you must begin with the end in mind—you must be able to picture clearly what this relationship will look like. You must know the qualities that you and your future partner must have to make your dream relationship a reality. You'll need to establish a "never compromise" attitude about your relationships; you'll have to learn how to identify negative relationships at an early stage; and you must be willing to end a relationship as soon as you learn it doesn't possess the qualities necessary for happiness.

This book is designed to help you do all of this.

I believe that in large part, the marriages that fail do so because the people involved have made a mess of the selection process. Most people don't have a clear idea of what they are looking for in a relationship. They hope that somehow when they're in the right relationship, the love bug will bite them and they'll know that this is the real thing. Such thinking invariably leads to disaster.

## The problem with dating

The Western, industrialized world is still pretty much unique in its reliance on dating for the purpose of mate selection. In most of the world, marriages are arranged; parents do the choosing, and following the wedding, the couple must get to know each other and learn to share life together.

## Why Date?

People haven't been dating all that long—only for the past century or so. But now it's a common part of everyday life in the Western world, and great sums of money and large amounts of time are spent on dating—to say nothing of the thousands of songs, movies, and books people have produced about this practice.

I believe that many marriages turn out badly because couples have dated badly. Learning to date more intelligently can produce a much greater chance for success in finding a fulfilling relationship.

What's dating supposed to do?

I believe dating can serve a number of positive purposes. First, it provides an opportunity to learn how to interact with the opposite sex. Social interaction and even conversation between men and women is challenging at best. Dating can provide an opportunity to hone these skills. Guys learn how to talk about something other than video games, cars, or sports. And girls learn how to converse intelligently about things that might be of some interest to the opposite sex.

People can also learn conflict resolution skills through dating. The sexes tend to deal with conflict differently. Learning how the opposite sex deals with conflict can be of great value for marriage.

Dating can also be a source of fun and recreation. Don't discount this aspect of dating. Life can be pretty dull if everything revolves around work or if the only social interaction you experience is with same-sex friends.

But the most important function of dating is mate selection. However, after approximately thirty years as a counselor and a pastor, I've concluded that either dating is a very poor method of mate selection or people don't know how to make it work. Since I won't be able to convince society to dump dating as a method for finding a mate, perhaps I can help by sharing some basic principles that, if employed consistently, will vastly improve the effectiveness of dating. To that end I offer what I have modestly titled *The Irrefutable, Irrevocable, Unalterable . . . Laws of Dating*.

I believe that most people who date either fail to understand basic relationship principles or are unaware that such principles exist. Whether or not people are aware of these principles, however, when they violate them, the results can be disastrous. On the other hand, when they follow these principles, their relationships have a far better chance of surviving and perhaps of becoming mutually fulfilling. People are much more likely to find a suitable mate if they choose to date intelligently. And not only will mate selection be more successful but the process of dating itself will be far more satisfying.

While you may not agree with all of the laws of dating, please remember that I have based these laws on decades of research by some of today's most qualified authorities on relationships. I've also attempted to base the laws on another, very important source of information about positive relationships—the Bible.

The laws of dating apply regardless of the age of those who are dating. People in their sixties who violate these laws can have just as devastating results as those who are in their teens and twenties. The laws apply regardless of one's socio-economic status, race, gender, or age.

Please consider these laws prayerfully. Don't discard any of them at first glance. Discuss each one with someone you trust—someone who has demonstrated wisdom and relational success. I haven't written these dating laws to spoil your fun. I offer them in the hope of sparing you as much pain as possible, both now and in years to come.

# The Laws

### Law #1
### *If it isn't easy and it isn't fun, break up!*

Once, a young couple who had been dating for a little over a year said to me, "You've just got to help us. We've struggled so hard to keep this relationship together. It seems that every time we turn around we have a new challenge, but we're committed to making this thing work."

I said, "Why?"

The question shocked them.

I continued, "Why would you work so hard to keep this relationship? Thus far you have proven one inescapable fact: Maintaining a relationship between the two of you is difficult. I'd advise you to break up and find someone with whom maintaining a relationship is easy."

The couple was stunned, but as we talked further they began to understand.

I wouldn't advise a married couple to end a difficult relationship. Those who are married should spend the time necessary to make their marriage work even though doing so requires a struggle. They've made a commitment, and they should honor that commitment.

But while couples who are dating may make a certain level of commitment, that's not the same as the genuine commitment of marriage. Lawyers and courts don't ordinarily involve themselves in the breakup of dating relationships. There is no formal commitment to dissolve when a dating relationship breaks up. Dating relationships are designed to be temporary relationships and should be viewed as such.

So, when you discover that a dating relationship is going to be difficult to maintain, you should dissolve it. Don't spend a great deal of time trying to repair it. Learn which of your partner's personality traits, values, beliefs, or life circumstances made it difficult for the two of you to be in relationship and then date someone who doesn't have those characteristics.

Marriage won't suddenly make it easier to get along with the person you are currently dating. In fact, the pressure increases significantly in marriage, making it even more difficult to cope with someone to whom you are not well matched.

Why would you want to spend the rest of your life exerting most of your energy just to keep your marriage alive? Why wouldn't you want to marry someone with whom it is easy to be in relationship and then dedicate your emotional, mental, and physical resources to some other, more creative activity or just to making your marriage deeper and more fulfilling than you ever believed possible? Wouldn't it be great to have an extra reserve of energy and creativity to devote to raising a family or excelling at a career? You won't have those reserves if you deplete all of them in simply trying to maintain civility in a marriage.

Sometimes dating relationships are difficult because one of the partners cheats. If the two of you have an agreement to date exclusively and one party violates that commitment, it's unwise to spend a great deal of time attempting to repair the relationship. Why? Because that person has proven that he or she will cheat. A person who will cheat on a commitment to date exclusively will likely also cheat in marriage. Why spend valuable time trying to repair a relationship that, if carried to marriage, will put you at great risk?

*The Laws*

If your partner is very needy and requires inordinate amounts of attention, you need to realize that those requirements won't be reduced if you get married. The problem exists on a deep level, and marriage won't solve it. Needy people should discover what's causing their neediness and then find healing before they date seriously—and certainly before they marry.

Law number one doesn't mean that a couple should never face a challenge together. Conquering a relationship challenge can bring two people closer to each other. However, when you must spend an inordinate amount of time working out problems, the relationship can't be considered as being either easy or fun, and it should end.

**Your own issues**

Some people have challenged me regarding this law. They say that if people run from difficult relationships, they'll never resolve their own issues. They claim that often when we find it difficult to be in a relationship with a person, it isn't because that person is flawed but because we are flawed. We carry our own negative emotional baggage with us into each relationship, and until that baggage is unpacked, we'll never be fit for meaningful relationships with anyone.

While it's true that we may be 50 percent or more of the problem in a difficult dating relationship, that doesn't necessarily mean that it's better to work out our difficulties while we're in the relationship. A difficult dating relationship will only slow down the process of our own personal growth. In most cases it is better to deal with these problems while not dating anyone steadily. Negative dating relationships require so much energy that we're often too tired to address our personal issues properly. We can progress more rapidly when our energies aren't divided, when we're free to focus all our energy on self-improvement.

Additionally, a challenging dating relationship complicates

dealing with personal problems. While working on personal problems, we're often confused as to which ones are relationship problems and which ones are personal problems that would exist even when we're not in a relationship. Without the relationship issues, we can accept personal responsibility for the problems that remain and deal with them unencumbered by the confusing maze of issues that so often accompany unhealthy dating relationships.

Some emotional damage or negative personality traits are so deeply embedded in our lives that they may require us to seek the help of a professional to identify and correct. There is no shame in seeking such help. It would be a shame to have the opportunity to experience a happier, more fulfilling life and never avail yourself of the help that is available. How much better it is to get the help that will enable you to enjoy life and relationships to the fullest!

So, deal with your personal relationship problems first and then date. You'll find that when you do so, you'll be attracted to healthier people and you'll be more attractive to the people with whom a relationship is easy and fun. And when problems do arise in the relationship, you'll be able to identify them as relationship problems rather than personal problems.

I believe that every relationship should be held loosely. Clinging to a relationship out of the fear of losing someone can actually bring about the result that you fear. The partner feels trapped and may attempt to create some distance from the clinging partner. When people become "clingy," they tend to suffocate the object of their affection.

Clinging also suggests desperation, and generally, desperate people are needy people. Often they have a low self-image, believe that no one could possibly love them just as they are, and fear rejection. Desperate people will do almost anything to avoid rejection. They'll plead, beg, change their behavior, and attempt to change their personality. They may even allow themselves to be treated poorly in order to avoid the pain of losing a relationship.

Maintaining a relationship with a desperate person requires a great deal of time and energy, which tends to drain the joy from the relationship. It's far better to be confident enough of oneself to be able to hold a relationship loosely. That means that you always give the other person an easy out. You may express such an out like this: "I don't know where this relationship is headed, but I know I really like you. However, if you ever decide that you are unhappy, just say the word and I'm gone."

Not only does providing an easy out remove pressure from your partner, it also places you in a position of strength. Before someone can love you, they must first respect you. How can they respect you if you don't respect yourself enough to release your partner when they tell you the relationship is over?

Healthy people are attracted to healthy people, and healthy people tend to be strong, self-reliant, confident, and independent. They don't expect a relationship to make them happy—they *are* happy people, and they bring that happiness to their relationships. Such people are almost irresistible!

## Best chance of reconciliation

When you give your partner space, you're actually providing the best chance of reconciliation. People find this hard to believe, but it's true. Giving the person who ends the relationship space immediately puts you in a position of strength and makes you more attractive. It also gives that person immediate feedback on what life without you will be like. This may be the most compelling argument for him or her to seek reconciliation.

By the way, just *saying* that you will give your dating partner an easy out isn't sufficient. You must be willing to do just that. If your partner ends the dating relationship, it is far better to let him or her go. Don't phone your former partner. Don't "accidentally" bump into your former partner in places you know he or she frequents. Don't beg for another chance. Don't write letters pouring out your lonely heart. And don't ask a friend to mediate a reconciliation. Give your partner space. If he or she initiates a contact, respond in a friendly manner without making it appear that you are anxious that the relationship resume.

Once while I was in college, I believed I had found the girl of my dreams. I just knew that we were meant for each other and that life together would be great. I was so anxious to marry this girl that I failed to notice how much energy we were expending to keep our relationship alive. Sentimentality had surpassed logic, leaving me vulnerable to making a potentially disastrous mistake.

This young woman was much wiser than I, and she chose to end the relationship. Quite frankly, she dumped me! Although she attempted to be kind in her choice of words, I found them to be unbelievably painful. But I accepted her decision, and we went our separate ways.

As devastating as that experience was at the time, it was actually the best thing that could have happened. Looking back, I realize that we were poorly matched and maintaining a marriage would have required even greater levels of energy from both of us. We both would have been left with depleted emotional, mental, and spiritual resources. While we may have avoided divorce, our creativity would have been sapped, and life would have been far more difficult. I owe a great debt to this woman. She was wise enough to sense that something wasn't right and strong enough to take the proper steps to end the pain.

Some months later I asked another girl for a date. I was amazed by how much fun we had and by how easy it was to be in a relationship with her. Every encounter was a joy. We never played psychological games with each other but were totally up-front with our emotions and thoughts. The relationship blossomed almost effortlessly, and soon I asked her to be my wife. As of this writing, Gayle and I have been happily married for more than thirty years!

For me, being married to Gayle is as fun and easy as dating her was. While life has posed its problems, the difficulties between us have been small, requiring low levels of energy for resolution.

# Law #2
## *Date only people whom you would consider marrying.*

The first law of dating can save many a heartache. Remember: If it's not easy and it's not fun, break up! My ex-girlfriend followed that law, and both of us were blessed by her decision.

If a primary purpose of dating is mate selection, then it makes sense to restrict your dating to people who might qualify as marriage candidates. Since you will likely marry someone you date, you provide a measure of safety by keeping that group rather small and excluding those who wouldn't make a suitable marriage partner.

So, how do you decide whom you'll date and whom you won't? Begin by asking yourself what you should look for in a mate. What characteristics do you desire in the person with whom you expect to spend the rest of your life? If you haven't made such a list, I suggest you get started right away.

When you make a list of desired characteristics for a future mate, it may be helpful to include at least two categories: negotiable and non-negotiable. Some characteristics may be nice to have but not absolutely necessary. Others must be absolutely non-negotiable. If a candidate doesn't possess one of your non-negotiable characteristics, move on. Don't waste your time dating people who wouldn't make a suitable marriage partner.

## Laws *of Dating*

If you are dating people who don't possess your absolutely non-negotiable characteristics, you are placing yourself at great peril. You run the risk of falling in love with someone with whom you're unlikely to find long-term happiness and fulfillment in marriage. I've seen people make a bad choice for marriage simply because they dated the wrong people and then when feelings of love grew, those feelings overwhelmed their thinking. The course of greatest safety is to identify the absolutely non-negotiable characteristics you require in a marriage partner and then refuse to date anyone who doesn't possess all of them.

What should you include on your list of non-negotiable characteristics? Allow me to suggest a couple. If you are a fully devoted follower of Jesus Christ, you should marry someone who is also fully committed to Him. Scripture warns us, "Do not be yoked together with unbelievers. For what do righteousness and wickedness have in common? Or what fellowship can light have with darkness?" (2 Corinthians 6:14, NIV).

Spirituality is the most important aspect of a believer's life. If two people don't share a level of intimacy on spiritual issues, how can they ever hope to achieve genuine intimacy in other areas of life? If you don't agree on the very core of life, how close can you two become? I can point you to many, many people who attend church alone, having married someone who doesn't share their faith. While this may not doom a marriage to failure, it certainly can place undue stress on it and can even result in pressure to compromise one's faith.

Some have tried to justify dating people who don't share their faith in Christ by saying they'll date them so they can witness to them and bring them to Christ. While you may be able to point to someone who was successful in such an attempt, most people fail miserably. In fact, it is much more likely that rather than converting their dating partner to Christianity, the Christians will end up compromising their own beliefs and values. Evangelism by dating is a very bad idea. Witness while you are just friends, but refuse to date anyone who doesn't share your commitment to Christ.

## A step further

Let's take this a step further. If you are a fully devoted follower of Jesus Christ, not only should the person you marry be a fully devoted follower of Jesus Christ too, but that person should also hold some specific areas of religious practice in common with you.

For example, I'm a Seventh-day Adventist Christian. That means, among other things, that I attend church on Saturday instead of Sunday. While on the surface this may appear to some to be a small matter, let me assure you that this can be a major stumbling block to a successful marriage. If one marriage partner attends church on Saturday and the other on Sunday, both will find themselves attending church alone. This practice isn't conducive to a satisfying marriage.

Some agree to go to church on both Saturday and Sunday, but that rarely lasts more than a few months. Others agree to respect their partner's religious practices while holding on to their own, but this can be less than satisfying since your partner rarely shares your experiences of spiritual growth. This can cause you to grow apart. Still others live with an uneasy truce in religious matters. This is most unsatisfying.

If they're lucky, the mixed-faith couple may have few conflicts over this issue early in their marriage. The real trouble comes when children arrive on the scene. Then the question becomes in which denomination will the couple raise their children.

If the couple chooses to go together to the church that one of them belongs to, the one whose church was rejected often feels resentment about the choice. So, some couples agree to choose neither denomination, thinking they'll allow the children to make their own decision when they're old enough. However, research shows that children from such unions rarely choose either denomination.[1] Most often, they're so confused that they tend to remain unchurched as adults.

When mixed-faith parents decide that the children will be raised in the denomination of one of them while the other parent will continue to attend his or her own church, the children are left at great peril. Research demonstrates that children who attend church with only one parent are at increased risk of dropping out of church as adults.[2] They are at greatest risk of doing so if they attend with only the mother, and at a slightly lower risk if they attend only with the father. However, in neither scenario are children as likely to continue attending church when they're adults as when both mother and father attend church together with their children.

So, if you date people who either don't share your faith in Christ or whose religious practices are significantly different from your own, you are taking a huge risk. I urge you to make faith in Christ a non-negotiable in dating partners as well as in a future mate. I also urge you to choose someone of your denomination whose religious practices are similar to your own. In matters of faith, the more similarities, the better for creating strong marriages.

A related area of non-negotiable factors is that of values. Our values govern how we live our lives. They affect the choices we make. And it isn't just the big choices that are affected; life principles and values also greatly influence small, everyday choices. It is important that marital partners hold as many values as possible in common. If one spouse values material wealth and the other spouse values family commitment, for instance, the result can be a high degree of incompatibility.

In subsequent laws we'll cover other areas that should be considered non-negotiable. For now, suffice it to say that you must compile a list of non-negotiable characteristics for your future mate and that as soon as it becomes apparent that the person you are dating doesn't possess one of these characteristics, you must stop dating them. Restrict your dating life to those people whom you would consider marrying. Don't place yourself at risk of falling in love with someone who would be an unsuitable mate.

# Law #3
## *If your dating partner uses/abuses alcohol, prescription medications, illegal drugs, or mind/mood altering substances of any kind, break up!*

This law qualifies as a non-negotiable for a future mate. Why? When people begin to use or abuse alcohol or any other legal or illegal drug, their emotional development stops that very day. A forty-year-old who began to use alcohol or drugs at age fifteen and is still using them is still a fifteen-year-old emotionally. While it is fine to think like a fifteen-year-old when one is a teenager, it really stinks when one is supposed to be an adult. Fifteen-year-old kids make lousy marriage partners. Add to this the fact that addicts fall into very unhealthy patterns of relationship, and you have a prescription for disaster in a marriage. It often takes years of intense work in recovery before an addict is safe to marry.

I've worked as a chaplain in drug and alcohol rehabilitation hospitals, and I can tell you that few things can have a more negative impact on relationships than addictions. Living with an addict can easily make you an enabler. Your love becomes sick—something we often hear referred to as co-dependency. The addict needs to feel your love by being rescued, and eventually, you learn to demonstrate your love by rescuing.

Addicts consider the substance of choice as the most important thing in their life. While they may say that you are more important to them than anything, their drug of choice will always take priority. In essence, they have chosen their lover, and it isn't you.

People have told me that they continue to date an addict in order to help him or her. This is always a bad idea. Dating relationships are not designed to rescue people with addictions. In fact, such relationships almost always damage the emotional health of the people who are attempting the rescue. The relationship changes the fabric of their love. They can find themselves retreating from healthy love relationships as they're drawn to an unhealthy, co-dependent style of love.

Those who are in deep relationship with an addict often feel they have to keep the dirty little secret. They find themselves making excuses for their partner or even lying for them while glossing over the negative impact the addiction is having. They may feel pretty good immediately after having rescued or protected their partner, but it's a terrible way to live one's life.

Should you marry an addict, you could very well spend the rest of your life rescuing your mate. Where will you find the energy to do anything creative with your life? Where will you find the energy to raise a family or to have a meaningful relationship with Jesus if you spend all your energies protecting or rescuing the addict?

## More than alcohol and drugs

By the way, chemical substances aren't the only things that can cause destructive addictions. Sex, gambling, shopping, and even video games can become addictive. And in recent years I've seen a dramatic increase of marital difficulties caused by one partner's addiction to pornography. While either party can become addicted, it is the man who is most likely to form a dependency upon pornography. The results can be devastating.

A man's use of pornography is demeaning to his wife. She feels that her husband is cheating on her and doesn't quite know how to compete with "virtual" girlfriends he finds in magazines, videos, and on the Internet. I've actually seen some cases where the addiction is so strong that the husband will turn down sex with his wife in order to watch sex on a DVD or a computer. The wife feels every bit as violated as if her husband were having sex with another woman. The embarrassment and feelings of worthlessness are difficult to measure.

Let me state this clearly: *"Virtual" cheating is cheating!* It destroys relationships and can be catastrophic to a marriage and a family. It reduces human beings to little more than objects of passion while ignoring personality, intellect, beliefs, values, and dignity. If you know the person you're dating to be a user of pornography, break up. You cannot help him or her beat the addiction. The addict needs to want to break the addiction badly enough to seek competent help and follow through with treatment.

We haven't even begun to speak of the other problems associated with addictions. These problems can include such things as financial stress, emotional distancing, loss of touch with reality, health problems, infidelity, extreme and persistent dishonesty, vulnerability to disease, self-hatred, self-harm, lack of dependability, suicidal ideations, and deep guilt and shame. This list is nowhere near exhaustive, but none of the things mentioned here are ever conducive to forming strong relationships.

Don't date people with addictions. Pray for them. Participate in an intervention with them, and get them to someone who can help them. But don't enter an intimate relationship with an addict. This must be an absolute non-negotiable for your romantic life.

# Law #4
## *If your dating partner is physically, sexually, or verbally abusive, break up!*

Let's get a few things straight. Abuse is always wrong. Abuse is never the fault of the victim; it's always the responsibility and fault of the abuser. There is never a time when abuse is permissible or even excusable. Abuse should never be tolerated or kept secret. God doesn't want you to live in an abusive situation. To live with abuse is not a sign of spiritual maturity. Those who abuse are unhealthy and aren't fit for dating, never mind for marriage.

This law is another non-negotiable. Abuse can never be tolerated. Physical violence, rape, verbal abuse, emotional abuse, and all other types of abuse are absolutely intolerable.

Statistics show that one in three teenagers have experienced violence in a dating relationship.[3] In dating violence, one partner tries to maintain power and control over the other through some kind of abuse. Dating violence crosses all economic, racial, and social lines.

Women ages sixteen to twenty-four experience the highest per capita rates of intimate violence—nearly twenty per thousand.[4] They're also at high risk for serious injury. They often believe that they're responsible for solving problems in their relationship and that they're to blame for the violence in the relationship. Often they'll offer excuses for their boyfriend's anger.

A young woman called me to ask about her boyfriend—she wondered what she could do to reduce his stress. I asked how her boyfriend reacted when he was under stress. She was very reluctant to tell me, but finally she admitted that he became verbally abusive and a few times he had even become physically abusive. This young woman was certain that she had caused him to react this way.

I told her that her attitude was the classic response of a victim of abuse. Victims tend to accept responsibility for the behavior of the abuser and to believe that if they could just learn to avoid making the abuser angry, the abuse would stop. It took some time, but eventually this woman began to see her boyfriend's abuse for what it really was—the behavior of a sick person.

Some victims have told me that they didn't believe the abuser would ever abuse them again. Pay close attention to the next two sentences: Anyone who has abused you is an abuser and has proven that he or she will abuse. The only appropriate response to abuse in a dating relationship is to break up immediately.

I'm not saying that abusers can't stop abusing. They can, but to do so, they almost always need professional help. You can't help an abuser by staying in the abusive relationship. Instead, if you stay, you'll develop unhealthy attitudes and behavior and will place yourself at risk for further abuse. This is unwise.

If you want to help an abuser, break up immediately and ask someone else to help you encourage the abuser to find help. Don't keep the abuse a secret. Secrets empower the abuse; openness takes away its strength.

Remember, if they are physically, sexually, or verbally abusive, break up!

# Law #5
## *Before you date, know how far is too far.*

How far is too far? I can't answer that question at any level of detail for you. What I can say is that you must set those boundaries before you date. When you're in a moment of romance or passion, it's too late to make that decision.

When setting your boundaries, it is important that you consider a couple factors. Consider God's principles for sexual purity. And consider the cost of failing to set appropriate boundaries. The cost can include such things as guilt, shame, unwanted pregnancy, and sexually transmitted diseases.

Don't think that you can't get a sexually transmitted disease. Every year, there are more than 1 million cases of pelvic inflammatory disease, 1.3 million cases of gonorrhea, and 4 million cases of chlamydia, and more people have come down with syphilis now than at any other time since the discovery of penicillin.[5]

# Laws *of Dating*

While the diseases I've just mentioned can be treated with antibiotics, there are many sexually transmitted diseases that can't be cured. It is estimated that fifty-six million people in the United States have an incurable sexually transmitted disease.[6] Twenty percent of Americans are infected with an incurable sexually transmitted virus!

One such disease is herpes, a virus that infects five hundred thousand people every year. And then there are HIV and HPV. You've no doubt heard of HIV, the virus that causes AIDS. HPV is the virus that causes genital warts and can even lead to cancer of the cervix. Some estimate that as much as 90 percent of cervical cancer is caused by HPV.[7] Cases of this disease are at near epidemic proportions on secular college campuses.

By the way, one study showed that condoms fail to prevent pregnancy 15.7 percent of the time annually, while another demonstrated a 36 percent failure rate in preventing pregnancy.[8] In addition, one study demonstrated that condoms had a failure rate of 31 percent in preventing the transmission of HIV.[9]

I haven't shared these statistics in an attempt to frighten you. However, the popular media is unlikely to share the results of such studies with you. They speak of sex with a condom as "safe sex." Those statistics don't sound very safe to me!

Certainly, it wouldn't be wise to ignore the negative consequences produced by failing to set appropriate boundaries for sexual activity. However, as important as this is, it's far better to set your boundaries based on positive values, and the best values to use when setting personal boundaries are God's values as expressed in the Bible. They'll never fail you.

## When your date disrespects your boundaries

When you've set your boundaries, if the person you are dating doesn't respect them, it's time to break up. Your boundaries are an expression of your values—of who you are at your core. Whoever disrespects those boundaries is disrespecting you. Mutual respect is a hallmark of successful relationships. It is unrealistic to expect that someone who fails to respect you before marriage will suddenly change and begin to show respect when you're married. This is why it's important that you break up with someone who fails to respect your values.

Many people tell me that those whom they date place a great deal of pressure on them to violate their boundaries regarding sexual intimacy. Some say things like, "If you love me, you'll let me!" There's only one appropriate response to such an idiotic statement: "If you love me, you won't push me to violate a boundary that's important to me."

Others say, "Everybody's doing it." However, the truth is that many people aren't doing it. Research reveals that the majority of teenagers and single young adults aren't sexually active.[10] But even if the majority were sexually active, how does that affect you? What the majority does or doesn't do isn't an expression of your values. Your values are just that—they are *your* values. No one has the right to push you to violate your values.

One young woman—we'll call her Jane—reported that her girlfriends were making fun of her because at age eighteen she was still a virgin. One friend was particularly pushy and gave Jane a hard time at every opportunity. On one such occasion Jane responded, "Look, I can become like you any time I want. But you can never again be what I am today. You can never again be a virgin."

Jane's response was right on target. A decision to forfeit your virginity is irreversible. Jane understood that and had committed to remaining a virgin until marriage.

But it's not just "the act" that Christians should avoid. There is much other "sexualized activity" that they should exclude from their life before marriage.

So where do you draw the line?

# Laws *of Dating*

I can't make a definitive statement for you, but I can share a general principle. My wife, Gayle, and I shared this principle with the young people in our church, and their response was very positive. (Gayle and I are both pastors in our church, so place our comments in that context.) On the question of how far is too far, we said, "Ladies, any part of your body that you would be uncomfortable showing to Pastor Mike is a part of your body that no one should see or touch before marriage. Gentlemen, any part of your body that you would feel uncomfortable showing to Pastor Gayle is a part of your body that no one should see or touch before marriage."

This is a general principle but one that I believe applies regardless of your age. Another way of stating this principle is the one-piece swimsuit principle. Any part of a male or female body that is covered by a modest, one-piece swimsuit is a part of your body that no one you're dating should see or touch prior to marriage.

Why is this true? Research shows that engaging in sexual intercourse or highly sexualized activity prior to marriage has a negative impact on a couple's relationship.[11] Allow me to illustrate.

Dr. Desmond Morris was a research psychologist who did studies of something that he called the "stages of intimacy." He has identified twelve stages, the last four of which I believe should be reserved for marriage. Dr. Morris's research indicates that relationships that either rush these stages or take them out of order are more likely to fail. The stages in order are: Eye to Body, Eye to Eye, Voice to Voice, Hand to Hand, Hand to Shoulder, Hand to Waist, Face to Face, Hand to Head, Hand to Body, Mouth to Breast, Touching Below the Waist, and Sexual Intercourse.[12]

Dr. Morris says that when these stages are rushed or taken out of sequence, the effect on the relationship is devastating. Eye to Body, Eye to Eye, and Voice to Voice can take place fairly quickly.

Eye to Body simply means that you see someone and like what you see. Eye to Eye infers some recognition through a look that contact has been made. Voice to Voice has to do with the first words that are spoken. My father's first line to my mother was "Hubba hubba!" You must remember that this was during the 1940s! Apparently, it worked—at this writing they've been married for fifty-five years.

Hand to Hand expresses a further step of intimacy. While holding hands may seem fairly innocent, it is inappropriate to hold hands with someone you don't really know. I hold hands with my wife, my sister, my daughters, and even my mother. After that, the list is very short. Holding hands expresses a level of intimacy that I don't have with many people.

Hand to Shoulder and Hand to Waist are further expressions of intimacy. Gentlemen, if you place your hand on the waist of a woman you don't know, she is going to feel very uncomfortable with how forward you are being. She may rebuff you angrily since you haven't earned the right to place your hand on her waist!

Face to Face is hugging and kissing. Certain types of hugs may be appropriate for people you know but aren't dating, but intimate face-to-face hugging and kissing is a level of intimacy you shouldn't share with many.

Many are surprised that Hand to Head is considered to be even more intimate than Face to Face. Truthfully, placing your hand on someone's head is crossing a boundary line of intimacy.

Everything else on Dr. Morris's list should be reserved for marriage.

The stages of intimacy are progressive. Rushing the stages or jumping over a stage in order to get to another one is a mistake and can have a negative impact on the development of a relationship. Engaging in any of the last four stages of intimacy prior to marriage also can have a negative effect on a relationship. One way of proving this is through the statistics regarding cohabitation prior to marriage. Those who live together prior to marriage have a divorce rate that is 50 percent higher than the norm.[13] Why? Dr. Morris would suggest that these people rushed the stages of intimacy, entering into the final stages prior to making a commitment through marriage. I urge you to make a commitment to sexual purity.

**"Re-virgination"**

If you've already crossed the line of sexual purity, it isn't too late to change your behavior. Remember, God can forgive sexual sin just as easily as He can any other sin. He will forgive you if you'll ask Him to. John tells us that the only requirement for receiving forgiveness is confession: "If we confess our sins, he is faithful and just and will forgive us our sins and purify us from all unrighteousness" (1 John 1:9, NIV).

When you confess your sexual sin before God, He is honor bound to forgive you. He promised He will, and to fail to forgive would be to break His word. God can't lie. He'll forgive your sin.

More than that, Scripture tells us that when God forgives your sin, He chooses to forget it too. The Bible says that He will remember your sins no more (see Jeremiah 31:34). And if God can't remember your sin, it's almost as if it never happened. Certainly, in God's mind it never happened.

God's willingness to forgive and forget is why I believe in "re-virgination." I believe that when you confess and are forgiven, since God can't remember your sin, it is as though you've become a virgin again. You've been re-virginated!

Jesus said, " 'Behold, I make all things new' " (Revelation 21:5, NKJV). "All things" includes you. He makes you a "new creation." When Jesus forgives, He also restores. So, don't lose hope if you've already crossed this line of intimacy. Claim the

## The Laws

forgiveness of Jesus and ask Him to "make all things new" with you. He can be trusted.

Today is the day to decide how far is too far. Today is the day to set your own boundary lines. Prayerfully determine how far is too far, and then commit yourself to live that way.

How can you make certain you don't cross your boundary lines in the future? Here are a few suggestions.

- Choose to date people whose reputation is one of having chosen strong personal boundaries and of respecting the boundaries of others.
- Double date or date in groups rather than single dating, especially when you don't know what value choices your date has made. This takes a bit of the pressure off. There really can be safety in numbers!
- Avoid spending late hours alone together. As the hour grows late, your energy and resolve weaken.
- Communicate your boundaries early on in the relationship. Share how important these boundaries are to you, and ask for cooperation from your dating partner.
- Don't use alcohol or drugs. They affect the part of the brain that controls judgment. When you are under the influence of alcohol or drugs, you are much more likely to make poor choices regarding personal purity.
- Begin your dates with prayer. This practice helps focus the will. Some may find it awkward, but it's better to feel awkward than to feel sorry.

So, insist on a slow, sequential progress through the stages of intimacy. Don't rush it! Taking things slowly can actually be much more enjoyable.

I've spent some thirty years as a pastoral counselor. In all those years I've never found anyone who truly regretted making and keeping a commitment to sexual purity. I have found many who have regretted following the other course. That's why this law makes sense. Know how far is too far before you date.

# Law #6
## *If either party needs to rescue, fix, or change or to be rescued, fixed, or changed, break up!*

The old saying is that on her wedding day the bride has only three things on her mind: the aisle, the altar, and him—as in "I'll alter him!"

It is a mistake to think that you can change someone. Don't date for the potential you see in a person; date only for what you actually see today in that person. Don't try to "fix" your dating partner. If your partner needs to be fixed or if you want to fix him or her, yours is a relationship in trouble.

Rescuing or being rescued implies a co-dependent relationship. This often happens in cases of addictions or in cases where one party has poor self-esteem. Some forms of mental illness or mental imbalance may also result in a person's feeling a need to be rescued. But rescuing is an unhealthy behavior, and needing to be rescued is also unhealthy.

I've seen some women hang on to a dating relationship long after it should have ended for fear of what would happen to the boyfriend. In fact, some men will even threaten suicide if their girlfriend leaves. At the very least he may say such things as "I don't know what would happen to me if you ever broke up with me" or "I wouldn't want to live if you ever broke up with me." If this ever happens in your dating relationship, you should see red flags, hear warning sirens, see danger signals, and hear alarm bells going off! The person who says such things is either unhealthy or is attempting to manipulate you into remaining in a relationship you may have outgrown.

You may feel good when you can rescue the person you're dating. Maybe you can get them out of their bad mood or fix their problems or keep them from getting drunk or using drugs. While this may bring some measure of satisfaction now, think about what it would be like to be married to that person. Think of spending every day of the rest of your life rescuing the person who lives in the same house with you. Think of never having space from that person. Think of all the emotional, physical, mental, and spiritual energy you'll have to expend to keep that person's spirits up. Is that really the way you want to spend the rest of your life?

In marriage, rescuing becomes draining pretty quickly. Ultimately, you can't truly love someone you don't respect. Can you respect a person who can't deal with daily life without being rescued at great personal expense to yourself?

Don't allow sentimentality to guide your thinking. If you think such a life would be acceptable, ask the spouse of an addict, alcoholic, or an untreated sufferer of bipolar disorder. Ask someone whose spouse has very poor self-esteem if a life of constantly having to buoy up his or her spirits doesn't get a little old at times. If those people are honest, they'll warn you against making the same mistake. Since the ultimate purpose of dating is to find a mate, you would do well to choose not to date people who fall into any of these categories.

If you are currently in a dating relationship with someone who threatens suicide if you end the relationship, remember this: That person is using suicide as a means of manipulating you, and you shouldn't allow him or her to get away with such behavior. While every threat of suicide should be taken seriously, such a threat shouldn't affect your decision as to whether or not to continue a dating relationship. Most threats of suicide are never carried out, and many of those that are carried out are carefully staged so the suicide victim will be discovered before it is too late.

Most suicide attempts are cries for help. Such a cry should be answered, but not by continuing a dating relationship. The answer should be intervention, professional counseling, and at times, perhaps even medication or hospitalization. Dating doesn't qualify as a suicide-prevention method.

Even if an attempted suicide is successfully carried out after a breakup, it is a mistake to feel responsible for the suicide. That act may well be a symptom of long-term, severe depression. There is no documentation suggesting that dating can prevent suicide or that breaking up can cause suicide. No one is that powerful.

Rescuing, co-dependent love is sick love and will never last. You can't afford to remain in a sick relationship. End the relationship, and then do what you can to encourage the person to seek professional help.

# Law #7
## *If either party tends to control, dominate, or isolate the other party from friends or family, break up!*

Controlling behavior, especially when it isolates an individual from family and friends, is often a precursor to abuse. This is dangerous behavior and must not be tolerated.

The desire to control, dominate, or isolate often grows from very poor self-esteem. People who control do so because they believe that this is the only way they can keep the object of their affection. They believe that if they allowed their beloved freedom of choice, their beloved would choose to leave—and they are desperately fearful of losing the object of their affection. They believe

*The Laws*

that such a major rejection would validate their worst fear—that they are so inferior and broken as to render them unlovable. Their fear borders on paranoia and can become violent.

Many controllers believe that in order to keep their beloved, they must restrict their contact with anyone who might encourage them to leave. Therefore, they think they must restrict their dating partner's access to family, friends, and anyone else who might draw their attention away from them.

I've seen controlling husbands record the mileage on the car's odometer and check it against the known mileage to the store, limit their wife's access to money, and screen the mail before they allow her to see it. Telephones are unplugged and removed from the house, cell phones are forbidden, and Internet service is disconnected. Dating partners may not have the ability to control things to that extent, but they still find ways to dominate and isolate the beloved.

Controlling behavior often presents itself in different forms, especially early in the dating relationship. Controlling partners may exhibit a negative pattern of communication that can be a warning sign of the domination that is to follow. They tend to interrupt frequently, stating their own opinions with great certainty and force. They tend to overpower their partner, not allowing them to express their thoughts, feelings, and opinions freely. It is as if their partner's opinions don't matter or they aren't smart enough to have a valid idea.

This pattern may exhibit itself in small matters, such as which restaurant to choose, or in larger matters of conviction, values, or faith. They may not allow their partner to complete a story he or she has begun but will interrupt them, correct their "mistakes," and finish telling the story for them.

When larger issues are at stake, disagreement is almost never allowed. If the partner states a different opinion, the controlling party will become adamant, stating his or her case in a loud, dogmatic, and even angry voice. And they state the opinion with such certainty that it implies that all other opinions are inferior or just plain stupid. This negative communication pattern invalidates the partner as being of inferior intellect. It says that their opinions just don't matter.

As destructive as this form of communication may be, worse yet is the controlling behavior to which it may be a precursor. As the relationship becomes more intimate, the need to control becomes more pronounced. Eventually, the controlled party may wish for a return to the "good old days" when the controlling behavior was merely verbal.

Controlling behavior is not just sick—it is dangerous! The statistics of thousands upon thousands of battered wives do not lie. These women know their safety—and often their very life—is at risk. Do not remain in a relationship of this nature. Don't just walk—run! Get out! Get help! Get away!

Love must be freely given and freely accepted. True love always carries with it the possibility of rejection. If my beloved doesn't have the option of rejecting me, it isn't love. She may be a robot but she isn't a lover, because true love is always a choice.

Those who control, dominate, and isolate have no idea what true love is. They can't give genuine love, and they can't receive it. Genuine love never forces. It always allows options, and one of the options it allows is that the object of your affection could leave you or reject you.

As needy as a controller may be, it is always a mistake to remain in the dating relationship in an attempt to help. The controller certainly needs help, but that help must come from a professional.

Don't settle for anything less than true love. Since those who control, dominate, and isolate aren't capable of giving it, don't date them. Pray for them, encourage them to get help, but do not date them.

## Law #8

***If you find it difficult to talk or to be accurately understood or if you find that the two of you avoid unpleasant issues in the relationship, break up!***

Communication is an important key to any lasting relationship. It is important that you marry someone with whom you find communication to be easy. Therefore, you should date only people with whom you communicate well.

What makes communication satisfying? First, mutual understanding should be the norm, not the exception. If most of the time you are misunderstood or you misunderstand your partner, your communication is neither effective nor satisfying. Mutual understanding provides increased feelings of love, acceptance, and value. Wouldn't you like to have these things in your marriage?

When communication results in fights, emotional outbursts, name-calling, or personal attacks, it has a destructive effect on the relationship. Words can wound or heal. The wounds may not be visible, but they exist just the same. No amount of "I'm sorry's" can take them away, and the scars can last for years. Satisfying communication is communication that is free of words that wound.

Satisfying communication always assumes the best. When something your partner says could be taken either positively or negatively, you must choose to interpret the words in the most positive way possible. Negative interpretations are extremely destructive.

People who communicate well have discovered methods of dealing with unpleasant issues and relationship problems that result in resolutions that are mutually satisfying. They don't avoid issues but deal with them in a timely manner. They don't withdraw from a discussion simply because it's become uncomfortable. And they don't view each other as the source of the problem but rather as teammates whose goal is to assist each other in finding satisfying solutions to the problems they encounter.

Satisfying communication is gentle, affirming, honest, and open. Those who find satisfaction in their communication can talk freely and easily without worrying that their words will be taken more negatively than they were intended. Resolutions to problems are found through open, honest communication, compromise, and teamwork. These are the things that make communication satisfying.

Drs. Les and Leslie Parrott suggest five rules for successful communication.[14] *First, make "I" statements, not "you" statements.* This helps you speak for yourself. It also makes your words sound less like an attack. Here's an example: "I feel disrespected when you give me instructions on how to accomplish the most simple of tasks."

"You" statements sound accusatory. It is better to avoid accusations and stick with honest communications of your own thoughts and feelings.

*Second, practice reflective listening.* Reflective listening is the practice of restating in your own words what your partner has just said. Most people fail to listen well. Instead of listening while their partner is speaking, they tend to be thinking of what they'll say when it's their turn or, if their partner's statement makes them feel uncomfortable, they tend to think of a defense or rebuttal. Reflective listening helps us focus on our partner's words. It helps us understand the words and the emotions associated with them.

*Third, understand and accept the differences between men and women.* Men and women think differently and even communicate differently. Linguistics expert Deborah Tannen says that women tend to speak in what she calls "rapport-talk," while men speak in "report-talk."[15] This means that women are usually more comfortable sharing feelings, while men are more likely to attempt to solve problems. Successful communicators learn to speak in a style that their partner will understand.

*Fourth, apologize when necessary.* A heartfelt apology can go a long, long way toward smoothing troubled waters.

*Fifth, communicate through appropriate touch.* Of course, appropriate touch changes as the relationship matures and grows in levels of commitment. Touch can be a powerful communicator, especially when you observe appropriate boundaries.

## How to handle conflict

Even when you're following the rules for communicating well, conflict is likely to arise. Successful couples know how to handle conflict. Dr. Susan Heitler offers a simple, five-step process: Listen to your feelings, describe the dilemma, make a request, listen to the response, and devise a solution.[16]

When a problem arises, it is important to take the time to survey your own feelings before you present them to your partner. Understanding the problem yourself will enable you to communicate it to your partner accurately.

Next, describe the specific problem and then verbalize your feelings about it. Use the five rules for communication we just examined, especially the rule about making "I" statements rather than "you" statements.

After your partner understands the problem and your feelings about it, you should make a specific request. Ask for a change of behavior, words, or attitude. Say something like "I would prefer . . . ," "I would like . . . ," or "I'd love it if you would . . ."

Once you've stated the request, be quiet and wait for a response. Make certain that you practice reflective listening as your partner responds.

Finally, devise a solution together. A real solution to a problem is one that works for both of you. Once you've agreed upon a solution, both parties should choose to give the solution their enthusiastic support.

Most problems can be resolved using this simple technique or a similar method of problem resolution. Effective communicators know how to resolve conflict creatively.

Research conducted by Howard Markman, Scott Stanley, and Susan Blumberg reveals that successful communicators avoid negative patterns of communication.[17] Relationships that have one or more of the four negative patterns these researchers have identified have a higher probability of failure than relationships that don't have them. In fact, removing one of the negative patterns of communication will do more to ensure the success of a relationship than adding five positive items. The four negative patterns that destroy relationships are escalation, invalidation, negative interpretation, and avoidance and withdrawal.

Escalation refers to a pattern in which arguments increase in intensity, volume, and negativity—perhaps even blowing up small disagreements until they produce major wounds that threaten the relationship. Invalidation is an attack, whether subtle or overt, on the feelings, thoughts, beliefs, values, or character of a partner. Negative interpretations occur when one party interprets what the other party says more negatively than was intended. And avoidance and withdrawal is the pattern that occurs when one party avoids the confrontations necessary to problem-solving. To make sure every communication has a positive effect, you must replace negative patterns with positive ones.

If you find it difficult to talk to the person you are dating, understand that marriage won't improve things. In fact, it often places new pressures on the relationship and tends to amplify the severity of the problems that existed when you were dating. So, it's important that you resolve communication issues while dating rather than hoping that you can work them out when you're married.

## Law #9
*If you've been the victim of molestation, incest, or rape, get help before you date seriously.*

Statistics on the prevalence of sexual abuse vary, but suffice it to say that in the United States, among women who have reached twenty-one years of age, somewhere between one-fourth and one-third have experienced some form of molestation, incest, or rape.[18] One study declared that 16 percent of men had also been the victims of a sexual crime in childhood.[19] In 1991, Sorensen and Snow reported a 322 percent increase in cases of child sexual abuse from 1980 to 1990.[20]

Add to this the number of young men who are exposed to pornography at an early age, and you have a picture of childhood in America that is quite alarming. Children in this country aren't nearly as safe as we would like to believe. It is sickening when those who are least able to defend themselves have experienced such unspeakable crimes!

Victims of sexual crimes suffer more than just physical harm. The most devastating effects are emotional, mental, and relational. Trust is difficult to achieve, and genuine intimacy seems impossible.

Guilt, shame, fear, anger, and even addictive behavior can dominate the life of the victim of abuse. Most victims internalize the guilt of what happened to them, even blaming themselves for the abuse rather than blaming the offender. They feel that something must be wrong with them.

# Laws *of Dating*

The guilt felt by victims is of several different varieties. Victims will feel "sexual guilt," which can continue into adulthood and negatively affect sexual relations in marriage. Sexual guilt is defined as guilt derived from sexual pleasure. Victims may also feel different from their peers, harbor vengeful and angry feelings toward both parents, feel responsible for the abuse, feel guilty about reporting the abuse, and feel guilty about being "disloyal" to the family and disrupting it. These feelings of guilt may prevent the victim from reporting the abuse, leaving the abuse an ugly secret that has great power over the victim's life. Research reveals that victims who keep the abuse a secret suffer greater emotional distress than do those who report it.

Guilt over childhood sexual abuse may interfere with the development of attitudes toward self, sexuality, and trusting relationships during the critical early years of development. If the child victim doesn't resolve the trauma, sexuality may become an area of adult conflict. When untreated, victims of sexual abuse are prone to crime, suicide, drug use, and, particularly in the case of untreated abused boys, are likely to become sexual abusers themselves.

Untreated female victims of childhood sexual abuse are three times more likely to develop psychiatric disorders or abuse alcohol and drugs in adulthood than are girls who haven't suffered sexual abuse. It also appears that untreated girls are more likely to become sexually active at an earlier age and to seek out older boyfriends, who might, in turn, introduce them to drugs. Eating disorders and incidents of self-harm or cutting are greatly increased in female victims of childhood sexual abuse.

Most sexual abuse comes from the hands of someone who is close to the victim, perhaps a close relative. The victim's issues with trust and intimacy grow out of this betrayal of trust.

Victims of sexual crimes, especially when the abuse occurs in early life, often require high levels of attention in a relationship.

*The Laws*

They find it very difficult to feel acceptance. They fear rejection and yet subconsciously expect that it will happen.

If you are a victim of abuse and any of this sounds familiar, you owe it to yourself to seek help. What happened to you was not your fault. You deserved better. What happened says nothing at all about you but speaks volumes about your abuser.

You don't need to live the rest of your life suffering these symptoms. Don't spend the rest of your life in pain. Healing is available. You can have a deep and satisfying relationship, but you must first find some resolution to the issues of abuse.

I urge you to delay serious dating and marriage until you have dealt effectively with the trauma of your abuse. Make certain you are able to give and receive love without reservation. You owe this to yourself!

# Law #10
## *Surrender your dating life and your sexuality to Jesus.*

Christians are fond of saying, "Jesus is Lord." In fact, the apostle Paul tells us, "if you confess with your mouth, 'Jesus is Lord,' and believe in your heart that God raised him from the dead, you will be saved" (Romans 10:9, NIV). This is a wonderful truth that stands at the heart of Christianity. Jesus is indeed Lord. But how can we say that Jesus is Lord if we haven't accepted His Lordship in every area of life?

Some people act as though they want to "protect" their sexuality from Jesus' control. They act as though they believe that if He's in control, they'll lose something of value or that sexuality will no longer be fun or fulfilling. This is utter nonsense.

Jesus invented the whole concept of sexuality. It was His idea and His creation. What makes us think we can improve on the Manufacturer's plan for this wonderful invention? We can't!

Every attempt to improve Jesus' wonderful gift of sexuality has always resulted in disaster.

Some Christians have denigrated and ignored the body, seeing it as "earthly" and therefore inherently sinful and even disgusting to God. They see sexual pleasure, even within the confines of marriage, as being a sin of the flesh or as very unspiritual activity. Nothing could be further from the truth. Sexuality is by nature a very spiritual experience. Students of human behavior have often observed that there exists a very strong link between spirituality and sexuality.

This link between spirituality and sexuality often comes as a surprise to couples who become intentional about sharing spirituality together. When a dating couple tells me that they intend to take their relationship to the next level spiritually by sharing worship and prayer time, I give them a warning. While I encourage them to follow through on their commitment to a deeper spiritual life as a couple, I warn them of the link between spirituality and sexuality. Many couples find that increased spiritual intimacy actually multiplies the desire for a physical expression of their love for one another. I know some couples who violated long-held personal standards of sexual purity after they began to share spiritually with each other.

Nothing makes a man or a woman more irresistible than the transforming power of the Holy Spirit. Your partner will be drawn to you as you are to your partner when the spiritual components of your relationship become more intense.

### The best lovers

One surprising result of a deep spiritual life is that deeply committed Christians make the best lovers. I don't say this irreverently; it's a documented fact! Just about every secular study of sexuality in America comes to the same conclusion: The people who are having the most frequent and most satisfying sex in

*The Laws*

America are middle-aged Christian women in long-term marriages.[21] Obviously, their husbands score very high in this category as well!

Secular researchers find this difficult to understand, but Christians shouldn't be surprised. People who are devoted to Jesus become more like Him with every passing day. One of Jesus' most important characteristics is unselfishness. Its opposite, selfishness, is the enemy of good sex. Unselfishness, on the other hand—the desire to meet your partner's needs first—is a hallmark of great sex. Highly spiritual people—those who understand and practice genuine spirituality—are often highly sexual people.

Never underestimate the strong link between spirituality and sexuality. You don't need to protect your spirituality from Jesus. Surrender it to Him, and He will give you the gift of greater and more satisfying sexuality.

Surrendering our sexuality to Jesus also means that we will accept and even rejoice in our maleness or our femaleness. Men and women are very different, and I say, "Thank You, Lord!" Accept this fact as a gift from God. Embrace yourself as the man or the woman God created you to be.

So, surrender your dating life to Jesus. Submit your choice of a date to His approval. Go on dates to places that He would approve. Engage only in those physical expressions of love that He would approve. Choose to make Jesus the Lord of every area of your life.

Some have agreed to begin every date with a prayer that invites Jesus to be the silent Partner with them. They report that this attitude dramatically changes the atmosphere of the date. They feel less at risk to violating personal values or standards. Hearing their partner pray such a prayer makes them feel safer and more relaxed on the date.

It only makes sense to make Jesus the Third Person on every date. If dating is the means by which we make such an important

## Laws *of Dating*

decision as the choice of a life partner, shouldn't Jesus be involved with the entire process? Don't you need His wisdom in making such a life-changing choice?

If Jesus is Lord of your dating life, you'll have fewer regrets at the end of each day. When you look back on your dating experience, you won't need to cringe or to hope that certain people have forgotten what happened. Guilt and shame will be eliminated. Your memories of dating will be pleasant. And if you've chosen a life partner, you can rest assured that you made the best choice possible.

Surrendering your dating life and your sexuality to Jesus is the most important thing you can do. It is more important than any of the other laws. If Jesus is Lord of your dating life, you will find yourself obeying those other laws of dating since Jesus leads us only along paths that take us to healthy relationships.

Make Jesus the Lord of your dating life today!

---

1. Dean R. Hoge, et al., "Adolescent Religious Socialization: A Study of Goal Priorities According to Parents and Religious Educators," *Review of Religious Research* 23 (March 1982): 26–304; Dean R. Hoge, Gregory H. Petrillo, and Ella I. Smith, "Transmission of Religious and Social Values From Parents to Teenage Children," *Journal of Marriage and the Family*, 44 (August 1982): 569–580.

2. William C. McCready, "Faith of Our Fathers: A Study of the Process of Religious Socialization" (PhD diss., University of Illinois at Chicago Circle, 1972).

3. Bureau of Justice Special Report: Intimate Partner Violence, May 2000.

4. Bureau of Justice Statistics, *Special Report: Intimate Partner Violence and Age of Victim, 1993–1999* (Washington, D.C.: U.S. Government Printing Office, 2001).

5. Stephen Genuis, "The Dilemma of Adolescent Sexuality: 'Part 1: The Onslaught of Sexually Transmitted Diseases,' " *Journal of the Society of Obstetricians and Gynaecologists of Canada* 15 (June/July 1993), no. 5, 556.

6. Felicity Barringer, "Viral Sexual Diseases Are Found in One in Five in the U.S.," *New York Times,* April 1, 1993, A1.

7. Barbara Reed, et al., "Factors Associated with Human Papilloma Virus Infection in Women Encountered in Community-Based Offices," *Archive of Family Medicine* 290, 2 (December 1993): 1239.

8. Susan C. Weller, "A Meta-Analysis of Condom Effectiveness in Reducing Sexually Transmitted HIV," *Social Science and Medicine* 35 (June 1993): no. 36, 1635–1644.

9. *UTMB News*, University of Texas Medical Branch at Galveston, June 7, 1993, citing a press release related to Weller, endnote 8.

10. "Teens Delay Sex," *USA Today*, March 16, 2005.

11. Desmond Morris, *Intimate Behavior* (New York: Random House, 1971).

12. Ibid.

13. Larry L. Bumpass, James A. Sweet, and Andrew Cherlin, "The Role of Cohabitation in Declining Rates of Marriage," *Journal of Marriage and the Family* 53 (1991): 913–927.

14. Les Parrott III and Leslie Parrott, *Saving Your Marriage Before It Starts: Seven Questions to Ask Before (and After) You Marry* (Grand Rapids, Mich.: Zondervan, 1995), 81–89.

15. Ibid.

16. Susan Heitler, *The Power of Two: Secrets to a Strong and Loving Marriage* (Oakland, Calif.: New Harbinger Publications, 1997), 107–125.

17. Howard J. Markman, Scott M. Stanley, and Susan L. Blumberg, *Fighting for Your Marriage: Positive Steps for Preventing Divorce and Preserving a Lasting Love* (San Francisco: Jossey Bass, 1994), 26–49. See this book for more details on these four patterns and on methods of identifying and removing the negative patterns from your relationship.

18. These statistics were given on the Women of Substance Web site: www.womenofsubstance.org/sexabuse.htm.

19. Ibid.

20. T. Sorenson and B. Snow, "How Children Tell: The Process of Disclosure in Child Sexual Abuse," *Child Welfare* (1991) LXX: 3–15.

21. Robert T. Michael, John H. Gagnon, Edward O. Laumann, and Gina Kolata, *Sex in America: A Definitive Survey* (New York: Warner Books, 1994).

# Breaking Up Is Hard to Do

I have a young friend who has little problem finding someone to date but has great difficulty in making a relationship last more than three months. Usually, by the three-month mark, either he or his dating partner breaks the relationship off. I've joked with him that he should write this chapter and title it "Fifty Ways to Leave Your Lover"! He says he knows at least that many. Truthfully, however, there is no easy way to break up. What follows, though, is some counsel that can diminish the pain of the experience.

Once you've decided that you should break up, it is best to do it right away. Don't put it off or wait for some magical time when it will be easy. Make the break right away.

It is best, in most cases, to break up in a face-to-face conversation. An exception to this might be if your partner is prone to violence or has demonstrated an ability to exercise extreme mental or emotional control over you.

Be direct and state fully that you want to end the relationship. Wish the other party well and perhaps tell them you will be praying for their future happiness.

If you have items that belong to your partner, return them without delay. Eliminate any potential cause for either of you to make contact. While a time may come when you can resume a friendship, in most cases that time lies in the more-or-less distant future.

Once you've broken up, don't initiate contact with your former partner. Doing so might send a confusing message. Don't do

*Breaking Up Is Hard to Do*

anything that might raise false hopes in your former partner that you might be having second thoughts. Make certain that every message is unambiguous. While you care for this person and wish the very best for their life, you are resolved that you won't be an intimate part of his or her life.

If the roles are reversed and someone breaks up with you, don't beg for a second chance. Honor their decision and release them. Don't make any contact unless it is absolutely necessary. This demonstrates self-respect. It also demonstrates respect for your former partner and his or her decision.

In addition, your having given the other party an immediate release when they broke up with you makes reconciliation more likely if it's ever to be a possibility. You don't have to be embarrassed that you've begged for more time. Instead, you've demonstrated yourself to be a person of strength and self-confidence. This is by far more attractive. However, let me share a word of caution here. I've never seen a strong marriage result from a dating relationship that went through numerous breakups and reconciliations. Such a pattern indicates a high level of instability in the relationship and should serve as a red flag.

Don't underestimate the psychological and emotional impact of ending a dating relationship even if the relationship should be ended and even if you're the one initiating the breakup. The reactions to a breakup can be similar to those of losing a mate to death or divorce, though not quite as intense. The loss of a relationship can result in sadness, depression, prolonged periods of crying, inability to concentrate, loss of joy, loss of hope, listlessness, irritability, loss of appetite or an uncontrollable urge to eat, sleep disturbances, loss of logical thought, and a sense of being distant from God—all of this and more over the break up of a dating relationship! You may find yourself longing for a resumption of even a painful relationship just to end the pain of separation. However, I firmly believe that as painful as this process is, it is still better than attempting to end a marriage.

## Recovering from a breakup

When you find yourself experiencing grief because of the loss of a relationship, understand that healing will take time. You may not be able to rush the recovery time, but here are some things you can do to facilitate a timely and healthy recovery.

First, tears are therapeutic. Don't hold them back. Let them flow freely.

Second, don't try to put the thing out of your mind. It is better to think through fully whatever thoughts arise. Some of the thoughts will be painful, and some may be pleasant memories. Think all of these thoughts fully when they come. However, test them by what you know to be true about the relationship, and refuse to believe things that aren't true.

Allow me to illustrate. If the pain of the breakup causes you to believe you are impossible to love, you must identify that thought as a lie. Believing that you are impossible to love may cause you to have feelings of worthlessness, shame, or guilt. It may cause you to engage in unhealthy behaviors, such as begging the person who has just broken up with you to take you back. Some people who believe this lie may engage in self-harm or other self-destructive behaviors—anything from promiscuity to extreme social withdrawal. You can identify a belief as a lie by examining the resulting feelings and behaviors. If they are destructive, then you can know that you have believed a lie.

Once you've identified a belief as a lie, you must replace it with the truth. The truth is almost always the exact opposite of the lie. In this case, you must replace the lie, "No one could ever love me," with the truth, "I am someone who can be loved and who is deserving of love." This truth doesn't ignore the fact that you may have personal and character issues that need attention. Instead, it acknowledges the fact that even with all of your problems, you are a person who can be loved.

So, again, an important step to recovering from a breakup is to think the thoughts fully, but we must filter those thoughts through the filter of truth.

Another helpful step to take after a breakup is to talk to someone you can trust. This should be someone who won't judge your feelings but will listen and offer support.

When you've found such a person, you'll need to tell the stories of how you met, how feelings of love grew, and how things fell apart. Tell all your feelings, both positive and negative. Talking is a positive step in recovering from a breakup.

It may be necessary that you talk to more than one person. You could easily wear out a well-intentioned friend. Spreading out the telling among several friends will help you avoid the possibility of making a close friend try to avoid you.

Another thing that can help after a breakup is writing. Keep a diary or a journal. I have one friend who writes poetry. Another friend, a psychologist, writes letters to Sigmund Freud! Whatever the form, writing helps organize one's thoughts and can be cathartic in nature. It may also help to wait a few days and then read what you've written. This may give you new insight on your thoughts and feelings.

Eventually, it will be necessary to declare your time of grieving over. Release the other person from your heart and mind and begin to look to the future. Let your thoughts be of a future of singleness. Make plans regarding what you'd like to accomplish with your life. Dream big dreams. But don't make the dreams dependent upon having someone in your life. Let that happen if it happens. Make the dreams about what God wants to accomplish through you.

Begin to think of yourself as a single person rather than a part of a couple. Form a new mental picture of yourself—a new personal identity. This is key to your beginning to move forward instead of looking back.

Once your new dream is in place, take action to fulfill it. Make a personal investment of your time, talents, energy, creativity, and personal identity. This is the final step in recovering from a breakup.

Breaking up is hard to do, but it is by far easier to break up an unhealthy dating relationship than it is to endure an unhealthy marriage or to go through a divorce. Don't be afraid to face the pain of a breakup if that pain will spare you the pain of an unhappy marriage.

# True Love

If the ultimate purpose of dating is to find a mate, it would follow that those who are dating are searching for true love. But what is love, and how do you know when you've found it? And once you think you've found it, how do you know if the love you've found will last a lifetime?

When dating, many think of only one aspect of love: *romantic love*. Dr. Larry A. Bugen has identified the characteristics of romantic love as being intense passion, ecstatic loss of judgment, obsessive focus on the beloved, desire for exclusivity, self-centered preoccupation with oneself, selective focus on positive qualities, exaggeration of real or imagined qualities, secret codes, private meanings, and special language.[1]

While some of these characteristics make romantic love sound like fun, they aren't enough to build a lifetime on. An "ecstatic loss of judgment" can't be good for long-term relationships. To experience a "self-centered preoccupation with oneself" means that you are focused on yourself and your feelings—your joy, your happiness, your passion. While this is fun, it is also selfish. In the long run, such a preoccupation will destroy the relationship.

Notice that romantic love has the double-barreled problem of a "selective focus on positive qualities" and an "exaggeration of real or imagined qualities." Choosing to focus exclusively on positive qualities means that you are ignoring the negative qualities of your partner. This could result in a rude awakening when the newness of the relationship wears off. "Exaggeration of real or imagined qualities" can leave you feeling cheated when you discover either that your partner doesn't possess the positive qualities you thought he or she had or that they possess the quality in much smaller measure than you thought.

As you can see, romantic love doesn't form a stable foundation upon which to build a relationship. If a relationship is to become fulfilling and stand the test of time, *committed love* must replace romantic love. Committed love acts very differently than does romantic love. Committed love is less inwardly focused; it has more of an outward focus. Dr. Bugen has identified the following characteristics of committed love: a mutual balance of met needs, other-directedness, realistic values and expectations, tolerance, yearning to be known, freedom to express all emotions, separate identities, and transcendence of two separate selves into one identity.

You can see that these characteristics differ greatly from those of romantic love. You can build a lasting, fulfilling relationship on the characteristics of committed love. People who have committed love also have passion, but they don't depend on it as the basis of their relationship. They know how to endure the ups and downs of a relationship while retaining the enjoyment it provides.

The characteristics of committed love are far less selfish than those of romantic love. Selfishness destroys relationships, while selflessness builds relationships. Committed love is a love that will last.

## The three components of committed love

Dr. Robert Sternberg has taken a deep look at committed love as it is seen in marriage. He writes that marital love consists of three components: passion, intimacy, and commitment.[2]

*True Love*

*Passion* is the longing or desire that lovers have for each other. It is the stuff of sexual attraction and romance and sensuality. Passion is the motivational side of love. Often it is stronger in the early stages of a relationship, fostered by a rapidly growing physical attraction. In Scripture, the Song of Solomon is written in celebration of the passionate side of love.

On the negative side, passion can also be possessive or even obsessive. Passion can move lovers to an extreme level of preoccupation with one another.

Eventually, lovers can incorporate passion into the bigger picture of love. Married couples can increase levels of passion in their relationship through meaningful touch, mutually enjoyable experiences, and through daily, heartfelt compliments.

*Intimacy* is the emotional side of love. Intimacy is simply knowing and being known. It is knowing a person well—knowing their thoughts, beliefs, values, likes, dislikes, and history. It means knowing everything—good and bad—and still accepting the other person for who he or she is. Intimacy provides that "soul mate" quality that so many seek in a relationship.

If love is to be fulfilling, there must be an open sharing of every aspect of life. Openness, communication, honesty, sharing, and support are all necessary for intimacy to occur.

People can increase levels of intimacy through spending time together, learning to listen to the words and emotions that their partner communicates, practicing unconditional acceptance, focusing on commonalities, and exploring spirituality together.

*Commitment* is a dogged determination to make a relationship work. It is the rock-solid promise to be there for the other person, uniting one's life with the other's, regardless of circumstances.

Commitment is the cognitive and willful side of love. It is the promise to be there "until death do us part." It provides certainty in a world of uncertainty. It declares, "I love you because of who you are, not because of what you do or how I feel."

# Laws *of Dating*

People can cultivate commitment in a relationship through acknowledging just how valuable this quality really is, through meeting their partner's needs, acknowledging their partner's commitment and sacrifices, and by making commitment a part of their identity.

Every relationship will have its ebbs and flows. However, for any love relationship to be strong, it must have a balance of passion, intimacy, and commitment. Having only two of those elements is something less than healthy. Those who have passion and commitment with no intimacy have foolish love. Commitment and intimacy without passion is companionship love. Passion and intimacy without commitment is romantic love.

Only those who have passion, intimacy, and commitment have true love—the love it takes to make a marriage last. Those who wish to build a great love should aim to grow each of these three elements. The more passion, intimacy, and commitment you have in your relationship, the better.

---

1. Larry A. Bugen, *Love and Renewal: A Couple's Guide to Commitment* (Oakland, Calif.: New Harbinger Publications Inc., 1990).

2. Robert Sternberg, "A Triangular Theory of Love," *Psychological Review* 93 (1986): 119–135.

# Finding True Love

How do you find the kind of true love, committed love, the previous chapter describes? How do you find the person you can love this way?

Here's the best answer I can offer: In order to *find* the right one, you must first *be* the right one. If you are looking for a mate, stop looking! Stop looking and ask yourself this question: "If I knew today that I would spend the rest of my life single, could I be happy?"

If the answer to that question is No, then do yourself and any potential mate a favor and don't get married. Don't marry until you can honestly answer that question with a resounding *Yes!* If you could not live as a single person the rest of your life and be happy doing it, you are subconsciously expecting that marriage will somehow make you complete—make you whole. You are expecting that marriage will bring you happiness.

Forgive me for bursting your bubble, but that is utter nonsense! If you are unhappy as a single, chances are excellent that you will be unhappy married. Marriage wasn't designed to make unhappy people happy. Marriage was intended as a means for two happy people to join their lives in the happy pursuit of a greater good.

The most important characteristic of a marriageable person is the habit of happiness. Learn to be happy today—right now, while you are single. Then and only then will you be a suitable partner for marriage. Don't take this counsel lightly—this may be the single

## Laws *of Dating*

most important thing I share with you. The most important characteristic of a marriageable person is the habit of happiness!

So, how do we do that? How do we find happiness? Allow me to direct you to some biblical texts:

- "Happy are the people whose God is the Lord!" (Psalm 144:15, NKJV).
- "Happy is he who has the God of Jacob for his help, / Whose hope is in the Lord his God" (Psalm 146:5, NKJV).

Do you want to be happy? Start with a relationship with God. The best thing you can do today to begin your journey to happiness and, therefore, to be ready to be married is to commit your life to Jesus. Confess your sins to Him, and allow Him to change and rearrange your life.

Statistics reveal that committed Christians report greater levels of happiness and contentment and are more likely to have a happy marriage. If you want to become a happy person, commit your life to Jesus. And once you have accepted Jesus as your Savior, it is necessary to make Him your Lord. That means that you will become obedient to Him. Solomon wrote, "Where there is no revelation, the people cast off restraint; / But happy is he who keeps the law" (Proverbs 29:18, NKJV).

You see, happiness is found not only in knowing God and experiencing forgiveness for sins but also in obeying God. If you would be a happy person, you must first know and obey God.

If you want to *find* the right mate, you must first *be* the right mate. You become the right mate by learning to be happy while single. Happiness comes from knowing God, loving God, and obeying God.

It is of equal importance that the person you marry shares your commitment to God. If it is important that you know and obey God in order for you to be the right mate, don't you think it might be equally important for the person you're going to marry to also know and obey God?

**Practice positive thinking**

If you want to be the right mate, you should practice positive thinking. Most negative people feel they could be positive if they lived in a better place or married a different person. But happiness doesn't hinge on better circumstances.

By force of habit, each of us is either basically positive or basically negative. Our circumstances change with the weather, but our attitudes stay the same. A person with bad attitudes will still be a person with bad attitudes, wherever and with whomever he or she lives.

Jesus said, " 'These things I have spoken to you, that My joy may remain in you, and that your joy may be full' " (John 15:11, NKJV). God wants you to be positive. Practice the joy of God in your heart, and refuse to marry anyone who isn't a positive, happy person.

During World War II, Victor Frankl, a twenty-six-year-old Jewish psychiatrist, was arrested and taken to a German concentration camp. Month in and month out, he worked under great chimneys that belched out black smoke from the incinerators where his father, mother, sister, and wife had been cremated. Each day he hoped for a few slivers of carrots or peas in the daily bowl of soup. In cold weather, he got up an hour early to wrap his feet and legs in scrap burlap and wire to shield them against the crippling cold of an East European winter.

When Frankl was finally called for inquisition, he stood naked in the center of a powerful white light, while men in shiny boots strode to and fro in the darkened shadows beyond the light. For four hours they assailed him with questions and accusations, trying to break him down with every lie they could think of. Already they had taken his wife, his family, his writing, his clothes, his wedding ring, and everything else of value. But in the midst of this barrage of questions, an idea flashed across Frankl's mind: *They have taken from me everything I have—except the power to choose my own attitude.*

You have that same power too. Choose to practice positive thinking. It is important to think positively about your mate. Instead of focusing on his or her failures, focus on what is good in them. You will find this impossible to do if you haven't established the habit of positive thinking.

In addition, it is also important to think positively of yourself. People who are critical of themselves don't make good marriage partners. God wants you to keep positive thoughts about yourself.

Romans 8:1 tells us that those who are in Christ Jesus experience no condemnation. That doesn't mean just that God won't condemn you. It also means that you shouldn't condemn yourself. Develop a positive self-image. Develop a positive attitude about life. If you want to be the right mate, you will practice positive thinking.

### Learn to adjust

What makes happy couples happy? Dr. Allen Parducci, a prominent UCLA researcher, asked this question.[1] He found that money, success, health, beauty, intelligence, and power have little to do with a couple's happiness. Instead, his research revealed that the level of a couple's joy is determined by each partner's ability to adjust to things beyond his or her control. Every happy couple has learned to find the right attitude in spite of the conditions they find themselves in.

Can you imagine for a moment how the Christmas story might have been written if Mary and Joseph hadn't had the capacity to adjust to things beyond their control? To begin with, Joseph had to adjust to the fact that Mary, his fiancée, was pregnant. He could have had her stoned or sent to some distant city. Instead, he chose to make the adjustments the angel suggested during his dream. He accepted Mary's story of being a pregnant virgin.

This couple interrupted their lives to go to Bethlehem to pay taxes. Mary, nine months pregnant, rode on the back of a donkey. Most women find it difficult to ride in a Buick when nine months pregnant, much less on the back of a donkey!

At night, they slept on the ground by the road. When they got to Bethlehem, the motels were full. Mary was worn out, emotionally drained, and at the end of her rope. When Joseph told her they would be sleeping in a barn, she must have almost lost control. But that night, the Son of God was born.

Mary and Joseph faced a difficult first year of marriage. After the birth of a baby Joseph hadn't fathered, they had to move to Egypt, set up housekeeping, and learn how to live with each other seven days a week. If Mary and Joseph hadn't been able to remain flexible and adjust to things beyond their control, the Christmas story might have been very different.

When I was young, I planned out my entire life. I knew exactly what I would be doing at age twenty-one, thirty, thirty-five, forty, fifty, sixty-five, and seventy. However, I have been 100 percent wrong at every age! Life hasn't gone according to my plans. I've faced more twists and turns than I ever dreamed possible. And when children were born into our happy union, the unexpected became commonplace.

A happy marriage depends on your ability to remain flexible and make adjustments. Expect the unexpected, and learn to adjust to life's surprises. If you would be the right mate, you will learn to adjust to things beyond your control.

## Only one shot

How do you find the right mate? You find the right mate by *being* the right mate. Practice the habit of happiness—a habit learned by knowing and obeying God. Practice positive thinking. Learn to adjust to things beyond your control.

# Laws *of Dating*

You may get only one shot at having a happy marriage. Don't blow it by trying to do things your way instead of doing them God's way.

Dr. James Dobson shares some further insights to finding the right mate.[2] Dobson suggests:

- Don't marry the person you think you can live with. Marry the one you can't live without.
- Don't marry someone who has characteristics that you feel are intolerable. In other words, don't bank on changing that person.
- Don't marry impulsively.
- If you are a deeply committed Christian, don't allow yourself to become "unequally yoked" with an unbeliever.
- Don't move in with a person before marriage.
- Don't get married too young.
- The stability of marriage is a by-product of an iron-willed determination to make it work.

Notice that all of Dobson's suggestions deal with things that are within your ability to control. He doesn't suggest that you depend upon fate or luck to find true love. Instead, he points to things you can do to increase your chances of making a good choice.

Finding the right mate comes back to the central point of this chapter. To find the right mate, you must first be the right mate. Make certain that you are the kind of person you would want your son or daughter to marry. That's the best way to find true love.

---

1. Allen Parducci, "Value Judgments: Toward a Relational Theory of Happiness," in J. Richard Eiser, ed., *Attitudinal Judgment* (New York: Springer-Verlag, 1984).

2. James Dobson, *Life on the Edge: A Young Adult's Guide to a Meaningful Future* (Dallas: Word Publishing, 1995), 102–104.

# Bringing It All Together

I have written at length in this booklet about breaking up unhealthy relationships. However, you should remember that the ultimate purpose of dating is to create a healthy relationship and to find a soul mate. You are much more likely to fulfill the ultimate purposes of dating when you keep the laws of dating. Violating the laws almost ensures that you will form unhealthy relationships and won't be able to find a soul mate.

When two people keep the laws of dating, they can discover that they have much more in common than they ever dreamed possible. They'll have eliminated the hassles most relationships struggle with and thus free themselves to devote much more energy to creating intimacy. They will discover a relationship that is fun and easy to maintain. Both parties will possess all of the absolute non-negotiables their partner desires. Neither will be hampered by addictions; neither will feel the need to rescue or "fix" the other; neither will attempt to control, dominate, or isolate the other; and neither will be abusive. Both will have the freedom from guilt that comes from establishing and maintaining boundaries for physical manifestations of love in their relationship. Communication will be easy and accurate, with both parties being free to express their hopes, dreams, values, and feelings without fear of rejection or judgment.

Those who keep the laws of dating learn that they possess a shared vision of the future. Their hopes and dreams are similar.

They find it easy to give of themselves in a relationship as they work to accomplish their goals together.

I have encouraged countless young people to date according to these principles. It has been my joy to watch the principles work. As a pastor, I have conducted many weddings for couples whom I knew had followed these important principles and were now enjoying the benefits of their hard work. While these laws offer no guarantee of happiness, they do offer the best chance for success in dating.

In addition to the laws, I would offer a few suggestions for making your dating experience positive. You'll find similar suggestions in James Dobson's book *Life on the Edge*. Here, I will summarize some of Dobson's suggestions and add a few of my own.

Look for someone with whom you have much in common. The more you have in common, the easier it will be to build a relationship. Similar levels of education, similar socio-economic levels, a shared faith, shared goals, and similar families of origin can be good starting places.

Take it slow. Don't let the relationship begin too quickly. Relationships grown too quickly tend to fizzle just as quickly. You'll have a better chance for success if you begin slowly. Allow the relationship to develop at its own pace as trust grows and you build a shared history.

## Feel good about yourself

It is always a mistake to confess too many personal flaws too early in the relationship. This can be misinterpreted as the result of low self-esteem. To healthy people, low self-esteem is a real turn off. Demonstrate instead genuine self-respect. Feeling good about yourself reminds you that you bring a great deal to the table in any quality relationship. A healthy self-respect won't allow you to be a doormat in a relationship.

*Bringing It All Together*

While it is important to be a servant, it isn't necessary to be taken for granted.

If the relationship has advanced to the point where you are dating each other exclusively, watch for signs of unfaithfulness. True self-respect expects that commitments will be mutually honored.

In addition, it is absolutely necessary that you respect your partner. Respect is a necessary prerequisite for love. Learn to demonstrate that respect by honoring your partner's values and boundaries without argument, keeping your promises, listening intently to what your partner says, and by refusing to rush the steps to intimacy.

You also demonstrate respect for your partner by deciding that you won't call too often on the phone—you won't smother your partner with too much attention. Both parties should speak respectfully to each other. And when you're apart, it is disrespectful to speak negatively of your partner. Respect for yourself and for your partner allows you to hold the relationship loosely. A man shows respect by holding doors open for a woman. While some may view this as a bit old fashioned, I find that women still appreciate a man who respects them enough to demonstrate that respect in time-honored customs.

Don't panic if the relationship is tested. Partners often test each other, especially if they feel this relationship could be taken to the next level. When this happens, don't overreact. Relax and remember to hold the relationship loosely. Don't cling to the other person—doing so makes you look desperate and foolish. It places you in a position of powerlessness. This is always a mistake. It also makes you appear quite unattractive.

Never express your desire to get married too early in the relationship. The only time to do this is when you can't think of any other way to break up, since it is entirely possible that your suggesting marriage will accomplish just that!

# Laws *of Dating*

As the relationship grows, make certain you re-evaluate it. Ask yourself again whether this person you're dating possesses all of your non-negotiables. Are you certain the two of you agree on important issues such as church attendance, how to handle money, how to relate to in-laws, who will work, where you will live, and whether or not there will be children and if so, how many?

Ultimately, there must be a feeling of comfort about the relationship. You must feel comfortable together. Shared values, goals, and a shared faith will contribute to that feeling of comfort.

While the ultimate objective of dating is to discover a life mate, it is a mistake to focus too intently on that end goal. Those who appear to be obsessed with evaluating everyone with whom they go on a date as a potential marriage partner will frighten away many good candidates. Relax and have some fun. That is a legitimate goal of dating, you know. Enjoying the moment will help you appear less desperate, and that is much more appealing.

Finally, trust your dating life to God. He can see the big picture, and He can help you find genuine success and enjoyment in dating. God wants what is best for you. Ask Him to take charge of your relationships, your social life, your sexuality, and your future. Observe positive principles of relationship and dating and then leave the rest up to God. As in all other areas of life, He will see you through.